from my front steps

ruminations, observations
and longing in a pandemic

joseph pinto

from my front steps
ruminations, observations and longing in a pandemic

Published by Distilled Press
Printed in the United States of America

Cover Design by Debbie Boettcher

www.josephpinto.com

First Edition

ISBN: 978-0-9991127-3-1 Print

summer 2020:

over the course of several days,
i took to my front steps with notebook,
pen, bluetooth speaker and
drink of my choice.

covid-19 had closed all my favorite watering holes
and where else was a barflypoet supposed to write?

so here's a little story about
ruminations, observations and longing in a pandemic.

i poured myself across those steps;
i never spilled a drop from my drinks, though.

from my front steps

the forgotten phase
wild bunny
lessons
clown
reaction
shut down
onlookers
she'll call again
two pages of do-overs
humid sunday
new normal
thunder
card dealt
outta nowhere
and beyond
birds
failure
electric sky
gathering drink, notebook and pen
chronic pain
pacifier
every
how deep is your love
figure out which
devotion
we all got played this way
crow haiku

statement from home
i feel it
inhale, let go
escapes
cutesy wootsey
so tired, still so far to go
please come over
prophecies and promises
torn open
not hungry anymore
i've something left
spirit and santa claus
up and off
weird couple
sticky and without reason
speed limit
god, please, cast me
lack of you
summer solstice
when will we be us
timing
purification
gazing westward
scared i might
prime member
nuts
reiki principle
italians
my path

if i'm okay
chemical resistant
ever wanted
sheets
like life
needing no assistance
be
haunted
back on the chain gang
my one (or a song swimming in bourbon)

the forgotten phase

the country closed tight
though like an old whore
some parts insist on creaking open
accepting the dime but not the dollar
common sense priceless and drying in jars
moonshine gone the way of lemonade
and the sober guzzle it
while the drunks measure the fingers
clinging inside the glass
laughing cause they get it—
the hard stuff lends the buzz
but reality is what'll get ya—
with swimming heads they toast the drowning
knowing thru abandoned hearts
they trained for the marathon
not the race.

wild bunny

wild bunny eats the grass so
i don't need to mow it and the
birds shit to remind me of all in
need of pushing from my life
and the clouds argue between
grey and white lacking thunder
and rain so desperately needed
to hide what's leaking from my
face and my drink is bottomless
even as i hit the ground and i
should go inside soon but like
wild bunny all i want to do is

run.

lessons

the frisbee creates
a clear division
in the sky

we laugh as
we drop it.

clown

the neighbors think
i own this smile.

reaction

*i don't love you
in that way
anymore.*

and my world squeezes.
and my sky collapses.
and my knees buckle.

shut down

airplanes go
where i cannot.

onlookers

they wonder what i am keeping at
those pigeons atop the peak
heads cocked curiously as
i'm writing my life out
and the motorcycles don't jar them
so my words won't.

she'll call again

like that you were done
no hitch in your voice
no tear in your eye
and across the line i felt you
basking in your coolness
but i bit down upon my tongue
to keep myself from saying
your fall will come.

two pages of do-overs

the words escape me some days
like you do
and i am left with pause
our possibilities seem ripe
but the vine goes unattended.
on these daydreamy afternoons
i wonder what it will take
to see harvest through.
at this point in my life
i've grown as tired of the do-overs
across this sun splashed page
as i have you picking me
only to leave me rot.

humid sunday

ninety degrees stains my tee and ass
i've run out of scotch and now
this bourbon is running out of me
the problem is i'm used to losing things
i've tried so hard to hold inside
maybe the reality is i'm the issue
solidifying with all my might
things that are meant to be liquid.

new normal

the bars have given way
to limestone under my ass
bands to a bluetooth speaker
and nights to full face sun

my drinks are deeper than ever
my attitude still giving two shits less.

thunder

when i was a little boy
my mother told me
thunder was only the sound
of angels bowling overhead
so when i hear it now
i laugh with the thought
we're all on one big alley
wearing miscolored shoes.

card dealt

the hanged man
so i am
self-sacrificing
desires unseen
by god's hand
dangling but hopeful
dependent upon
spirit's intervention.

outta nowhere

you write words from pictures.

i craft shit from my ass.

and beyond

little bug flies on my arm
i blow him away
to infinity.

birds

above the bluetooth speaker
i still hear the birds
they sing no matter these chords
subtle reminders
i'm grounded and connected
even while i float in space.

failure

i can pretend i don't need you.

i can pretend.

electric sky

stretching before me the latest front
pregnant in expectancy
(will she be short on arrival)
i beg you
do not spare me your birthing
beautified upon forked tongue
charged and sweeping

lash me into ascension.

gathering drink, notebook and pen

gloam reimagines my hues
my daughter waits within
a house i have brushed
with different colors
countless times and no matter the light
it appears the same;
i am as misplaced
within those walls
as i am under canopied acceptance,
and god loves me all the same

though i struggle to.

how i loathe gathering drink,
notebook and pen, walking in
wondering if she sees the division
in my smile and wondering
if she knows my eyes have long since set.

chronic pain

it's borrowed time sitting atop my front steps
no longer can my spine withstand the compression
i grit teeth and knock the amber down my throat
disconnecting anguish from reality
month by month bowing just a bit more
in my head i am still who i can no longer be
come stare into my eyes before they dull over
there before you the illusion i've married—
i am whole; i am whole—
but i am nothing. and i am tired. and i am worn;
the humidity rolling down my ribs
a reprieve to the fire rolling
thru my core.

pacifier

little boy with pacifier
runs up on foreign lawn
momma jerks him backward
haven't we been jerked backward
countless times
some get the lesson
others search for something to suck on.

every

every song i hear
an excuse to sing you
every line a reason
to bleed my heart
every word affirmation
you're here but not.

how deep is your love

we're living in a world of fools
the bee gees opened my eyes
drunk and singing

nothing could be truer.

figure out which

my feet are ugly
my mind beautiful
one needs a good scrubbing
the other just needs to be.

devotion

you're not with me
but i'm still there
with you.

we all got played this way

the kids play hoops
ball a heart
skipping in beat
perpetuating
dangers of the street.

crow haiku

crow flies high above
sun catches ebony wings
i wish i were it.

statement from home

they protest the injustices
spat from this world;

know little of their neighbor's anguish.

i feel it

kissing him
kills me.

inhale, let it go

i wanted to write.

i think i'll enjoy
this weather instead.

escapes

my daughter sits inside
living worlds in her ipad
i sit on my front steps
sharing mine in a spiral.

cutesy wootsey

i love the little bunnies
especially when i'm drinking
i make googly noises
aww you're such a bootiful widdle bunny
fuzzy cutesy wootsey widdle bunny

i don't care who's listening.

the bunnies know i'm a man grown
around a child's heart.

so tired, still so far to go

staring fifty down the barrel
trigger's cocked and i still ain't got
none of this life quite figured out
tired of cleaning between fingers
while the loss piles at my feet
my tongue remains insatiable
skin porous and eyes open wide;

the last bullet has been spun
in the chamber.

please come over

please come over
crack a beer
listen with empathy—

i'll tell you
i've been hurting
all my life.

prophecies and promises

my tarot spoke of a storm coming
but the weatherman didn't warn me
so i poured a bourbon and a beer
and took to my front steps hoping
to divine what the fine lines of
my uni-ball pen conjured
within a one subject notebook
lacking the muscle to support
the entirety of my complexity
something i have endured thru this
the celtic cross spread of my life
while atop the horizon goliaths gathered
churning in tease of prophecies and promises
i have waited for in unwavering faith
tortured by sutured lips of spirit
whose grand notebook far dwarfs
my own.

torn open

do you think you did me a courtesy
your olive branch of a final call
as if that honeyed voice
could explain the loss of love
make it all okay
thorned dismissal with no favors
a silence endured for weeks
heard your heels screaming
our reality too much to bear
do you still smooth your sheets
men leave their socks behind
but never their shoes
i had my winter coat packed
and poetry for you
i wish you had ghosted me
instead of exposing my ribs
horrible things are leaking
love and all that once bound me.

not hungry anymore

seems as though everyone's inside
chilling skin and protecting themselves
barriers come in cloth now
as if words did not infect enough
i sunburn my eyes
so i can't see what i'm thinking
my verse fuels visions and
in this heat paragraphs and booze
do not dispel reality so easily
dinner seems a welcome thought to fill me
so too, once, the thought of you and i
you made it clear you couldn't stomach that
and force-fed i had no choice but digest.
these days i am hardened but liquid
spilling quietly from the seams
and i can't smell what the neighbors are cooking
or tell you you've ripped out my guts
when i was quite content with the way
you stole my heart.

i've something left

pandemic and illegal fireworks
it's all that's plaguing us nowadays
distant pops rousing us from
sleepy newsreels stuck on a loop
while guards remain prudent
vigilant to thieves stalking both
air as well our minds
fourth of july still days away
but none of us lack
for sizzle or grilling
this, a summer made for discontent,
expiring to all manner unseen,
while i ponder who might join me
in one last burst of brilliance.

spirit and santa claus

spirit told me
at this point in my life
i should surrender
to the will of the universe

but july reminds me
of picnics i never attended;
i tell myself the invites got lost,

(while across my front walk
children ride scooters)
betraying the dark
i've suppressed for so long

i would think innocence smells
like rain and barbecues;
i was never allowed outside

this little boy struggles
with love never found;
summer arrives on the cusp
of my void yet still

still i fight for the magic
of decembers.

up and off

pull it up and off
these ain't scars
just the course of your love
you've been rough
i've paid no mind
i hold to the chance
you'll want me without
all that hurt again
i never asked for much
isn't that enough
to fall down, and get back up
again pull it up and off
you craved me bare chested
i left my shirts behind
your intentions outgrew mine
so you threw them away
someone's got me on their back now
it ain't the same.

weird couple

they're a weird couple, walking the dog
one much further ahead than the other
(while blissfully pooch sniffs about)
and their lips are unmoving
while my playlist fills in the silence;
carefully they are spaced
wearing neither mask nor affection
yet their love slows up their gait.

i sip my lemon vodka
wondering if it'd pair well with sweet tea
and if i could run the fuck away from here
without anyone noticing.

sticky and without reason

thick brushed my brow by humidity
clung to me secrets dripping
july flash storm throaty
grass blades alive and glistening
midafternoon in measures dying
i sit drinking.

speed limit

i like to watch the cars as they drive by.
the faces inside always turn and stare.
where are they going and
why do they speed on a residential street?
sometimes i want to raise the glass beside me
toast their recklessness.
the sentiment would go unappreciated though.
look at that drunken fool, the faces would say,
living it up as though he might die tomorrow.

god, please, cast me

gonna get myself good and wasted
happy hour sun got me baked
inside my head volume's up
i keep those drinks goin' down
if i drop won't feel the fall
concrete should straighten all that's bent me

broken bones are meant for mending;
you can't do shit for spirit.

lack of you

not the booze, not my pain—

it's the lack of you killing me
mourning this silent phone
your ringtone chimes in my head
and my inhalations are
the scent of your skin painted
by my tongue; i miss you,
a phantom limb born with me
and i am longing for reunion.
you're the better half of my worst
at my worst, you're best of all—

i do not want to die yearning
but knowing i am finally whole.

summer solstice

parched, my lawn burning
brittle, hay in structure;
i am speaking infernos
into my pad again
last night's misgivings
trickling down my back
and i will never be extinguished,
will i?
a wick
made for cold burn
robbed of embers
i surely have deserved
and i will never be snuffed,
god why?
let me burn out, let me burn out
let me burn down, die
grant me one season to blaze
suffocate lungs
so i am heard and
never spoken of again;
parched, my lawn browning
brittle, hay in structure.

when will we be us

you can't share my drink
but we can share the sky
do you gaze as i do
alone atop front steps
filling spaces with question marks
while the breeze exclaims
touch atop skin
and i am dumbstruck

and i am in awe

the further you draw
the closer you come in
you had me the moment
god made this world spin;
indoor living stifles the senses
but outdoors universe reminds:
we are tethered.

still hopeful the string shortens
lengthening our mythos.

timing

we don't ask for the things
that come our way
at least so it seems
i sometimes wonder if we're wired
a hot button planted by the universe
beyond our knowledge and recognition
drawing in devils when desired
while the angels wait upon our last breath
a cosmic s.o.s. till gasped

please bring me what i need.

purification

i can heal you.

but you can't heal me.

gazing westward

from across the street my neighbor:
you're still sitting out here
it's been hours.

if he knew of my void within
he'd be out here, too.

scared i might

i don't know if this is our story's end.
i'm still knocking on your heart;
i remember the day you opened that door—
you peeked your head out
wasted no time kissing me;
i wasted no time exhaling
every fiber of myself into your lungs.
i have not caught my breath since.
i am suffocating in our silence
scared i might live out my life without you.

prime member

top step digs into my ass
thank god for the cushion
amazon bestowed upon me
a thin layer of foam
comfort for the cheeks
life has kicked for too long.

nuts

squirrels digging into lawn
admiring their tenacity
i grasp my drink
and keep pounding.

reiki principle

as a boy i killed the ants
now i move them along.

italians

breasts one way, ass the other,
italian lady walks along my
front walk wearing a
dressier version of the
nightgown my grandmother
once wore and seeing me
hurries along, startled perhaps
by my presence, a paisano
thinking loudly of longing;
singing of a broken heart.

my path

sparrows shit atop the front walk lights
my path has been shit upon before
residue of all that's preceded
i wonder if it's karma or
what's meant to be
isn't it all the same
nature does what it will do
while we perceive
what we want.

if i'm okay

she's having her first sleepover
i can feel her glow from down the block
she's found a friend who accepts her as she is
it's all i could ever ask for
a lesson i pray she learns
without my constant reminding
it's hard being a father
trading football jersey for dolls
a stern tongue for princess voices
and i'd be a liar if i said i wasn't a bit sad
and i'd be a liar if i said i won't consult
the stuffed animals lining her bed tonight
hoping they'll ask in inflections i impersonate
if i'm okay.

chemical resistant

i stopped fertilizing my grass
instead invested into nurturing myself
weeded my head but couldn't keep
the sun from my heart
i'm in constant bloom
persevering thru the most
inclement of seasons
i die and grow
die and grow
resistant to your removal.

ever wanted

you may never read this
but all i have ever wanted
your footfall beside mine
down the front path
turn of key in lock
and my eyes smiling
baby, we're home.

sheets

solstice has passed;
already the day dips a bit sooner than desired.
the pillow cries from an awkward bedroom
where truth comes chilled by central air
and fevered ruminations dampen the soul.
no pandemic hastened this plight.
the cells die infected upon inception
and we struggle against karmic expirations
sweating thru sheets – and sheets of denial.

like life

if my dad were here
he'd show me
how to do things.

needing no assistance

if i puke
i'll puke in the street
so when the rains come
i'll thank the heavens
for cleansing what ills me
and the neighbors will speak
of the drunk on the steps
who stumbled with perfect vision
while blind.

be

wednesday is dying and from
between the railing cobwebs come alive
silvery nettings cast some late night
or early morn by many legged creatures
living in absurdly simple faith
spinning intentions and waiting
until their manifestations come to it.
they know no god no angel yet
instinctively surrender all expectation
and be.
hidden from sight the breeze dances thru
their handiwork and as
wednesday passes on i cry

teach me.

haunted

gone 13 years ago today
sometimes i imagine my dad a hawk
catching currents, screeching overhead
and no matter how much i drink
i still hear him crying.

back on the chain gang

i see angels in clouds
none on my shoulder
i'm so over the signs
still wanting for intervention
the pretenders are playing and
i'm wondering about the
reality of my life—
are you my truth
or a master fabrication
a way to get me
from this day to next—
i'm faltering without you
but i'm created
to toil an eternity.

my one
(or a song swimming in bourbon)

been others before you
might be more to come
but babe if you don't want me
know you're still my one

seen my share of storms
and i've been drenched thru
fought against currents
and turns of the moon
been waiting on your call
saying your running is done
but babe if you don't want me
know you're still my one

this dufflebag's been packed
and i got extra shoes
if airlines ain't flying
then i'm walking to you
don't matter the distance
or if i run out of sun
babe if you don't want me
know you're still my one

known heaven and hell
in this lifetime of mine
still chasing you baby
and mountains i'd climb
for the chance to be with you

for the chance at divine

baby you're my divine

seen my share of storms
and i've been drenched thru
fought against currents
and turns of the moon
been waiting on your call
saying your running is done
but babe if you don't want me
know you're still my one

babe if you don't want me
know you're still my one.

Joseph Pinto is the author of the poetry collections *From My Front Steps* (2021), *Scotch and Scars* (2020) and *A Distilled Spirit (2018)*, the poignant novella *Dusk and Summer (2014)* and the horror novel *Flowers for Evelene (2005)* – as well numerous dark fiction tales; his unique voice has been showcased in a multitude of anthologies and magazines as well as individually published short stories.

He is known as the barflypoet – and yes, he really writes poetry from inside bars.

Indulge in Joseph's work at www.josephpinto.com

Follow him on:

Twitter: @JosephAPinto

Instagram: @joseph_a_pinto

Facebook:
Joseph A. Pinto, barflypoet & author of dark fiction

YouTube (spoken word poetry):
Joseph Pinto, the barflypoet